FOR A MORE
PERFECT
UNION

By

John B. Bloom

Book Publishing Group LLC

42 Broadway 12th floor, New York, NY 10004

www.bookpublishinggroupllc.com

Dedication

This book is dedicated to the United States Constitution and to those both living and dead who took an oath to protect and defend the Constitution of the United States against all enemies, both foreign and domestic, including members of the Democratic and Republican Parties, and to future generations of citizens and residents of the United States of America.

President Andrew Jackson said, "One man with courage makes a majority." There can be no better description of Congressman Thomas Massie. Congressman Massie was the lone Republican member of the House of Representatives to join Democrats in calling for the Department of Justice to release all the Epstein files. After he successfully recruited enough Republicans to sign the Discharge Petition, all but one Republicans in both Chambers of Congress voted to require the Department of Justice to release all the Epstein files. I dedicate this book to Congressman Thomas Massie, in hopes that others will have the courage to follow him.

Table of Contents

Introduction

I would like to introduce myself to most of you. My name is John Bloom. I am sixty-three years old and retired. I have been fighting political corruption for over thirty years, in the New York State Conservative Party and the Republican Party of Virginia. This book is written to enlighten the American public about the corruption of the Constitution of the United States by Republicans and Democrats alike. At the time of the writing of this book, I am the Chairman of the Constitution Party of Virginia and ran for public office as a candidate of the Republican Party of Virginia, Constitution Party of Virginia, the Libertarian Party of Virginia, and the Conservative Party of New York and had over 20 letters to the editor published in newspapers across Virginia and other states, providing solutions to America's problems, not rhetoric. I have a Bachelor's degree in Nuclear Engineering from Penn State University and a Master's degree in Environmental Technology from the New York Institute of Technology. As an Engineer, I learned how to solve problems and incorporated what I learned as an Engineer to provide solutions for America's economic, social, and taxation problems. This book addresses the corruption of Political Parties, their legislation that has deviated from the US Constitution, and offers constitutional alternatives, making America a Constitutional republic again.

Discrimination Against a White Male – It Happened to Me

I was discriminated against as a white male by the US Navy when I was directed to perform work as a black female within the Dosimetry Branch of the Norfolk Naval Shipyard under the Command of then Captain Dianna Wolfson. I was a Federal Civilian and a former US Naval Veteran. This individual, who was known by just about everyone within the branch of avoiding work, including all members of the Radiation Health Division. A message I sent to a black female, then Deputy Director of Radiation Health, Lt. Tai Tuttle, requesting a meeting to discuss a transfer to remove myself from the Hostile Work Environment. That message I sent to my Supervisor, John Kupiec, and to Lt. Tuttle ONLY, was used by the black female to submit a Complaint for "Disrespect to a Coworker" and received a "Letter of Reprimand after I was granted that meeting and DENIED my transfer by Lt Tuttle. Then I sent messages to the Radiological Controls Director, Gary Sauers, to discuss appealing that decision, receiving the "Letter of Reprimand". Those messages were used by then Radiation Health Director Christina Turconi, a white female, who issued a five-day suspension without pay for "Disrespect" to management.

About that time, I received training on discrimination by the Equal Employment Opportunity office on discrimination. Then I submitted a formal discrimination complaint through that office. Then a series of violations of Federal Law occurred by the Command. First, the Command stripped me of my Security Clearance WITHOUT any review of the Navy Inspector General's office to investigate if the removal of my Security Clearance was an act of retaliation, which it was. After my EEOC Complaint was dismissed by an EEOC Judge and after I submitted my appeal, when reviewing documents that were submitted in the name of Secretary of the Navy, Carlos Del Toro, I discovered a fabricated document. The document submitted to the EEOC was a suspension for the same complaint she had made against me. However, the first page of that suspension letter was for parking in a reserved parking space she was told not to park in. The 2nd page which was signed by that black female acknowledging she received and understood the suspension. That date signed by that individual was "May 16th, 2022." The date was changed by

Ms. Turconi to "April 16th, 2022", which was before I submitted my EEOC Complaint and created the illusion that I was treated the same as she was.   I was suspended with pay and not able to investigate and confirm information at Norfolk Naval Shipyard, my supervisor, Mr. Kupiec, confirmed that this individual only had one suspension, not two. I believe the individual who signed that letter was unaware of the change in the document she signed that was submitted to the EEOC.

After that came the Unjust and illegal suspension of my security clearance, a suspension without pay that lasted from November 25th, 2022 thru July 30th, 2023, when I was terminated. While this ended my Federal Employment, Dianna Wolfson was PROMOTED to Rear Admiral, after several violations of Federal Law, which have never been investigated. I was denied my day in court and even filed a Federal Lawsuit against Ms. Wolfson and others. Though I made several complaints to the Office of Special Counsel, the Department of Defense, and the US Navy for acts of retaliation by Ms. Wolfson and company, there has been no investigation; in fact, the Department of Justice is defending those who violated the law.

To prevent this from happening to others, I recommend that a Citizen Organization be formed of diverse individuals with equal members of white males and females, black males and females, Hispanic males and females, Asian males and females who have been discriminated against.

Remove demographics from all application forms, just age and phone call interviews to prevent appearance, race, and gender in the hiring or promotion processes. No more quotas. Most companies will hire and promote the best-qualified individuals for a position if they are not locked into a numbers game. Federal and State Governments, which are not driven by efficiency and productivity, waste taxpayer funds by not hiring the best people, but are driven to protect inefficient workers based on race and gender. Denied my day in court, this book is my last resort to obtain American Justice for a more perfect union, where all Americans are treated fairly.

John B. Bloom

Corruption Of Political Parties and That Undermined America's Constitutional Republic

The corruption of the Conservative Party of New York State:

New York State allows voter registration by political party and permits cross-endorsement, meaning a candidate can be endorsed by and appear on the ballot line of more than one political party. However, voters do not evaluate candidates based on their adherence to the principles and issues of each party's line; this system has been subjected to misuse. In Suffolk County, New York, leaders of the Conservative Party received county, town, or federal patronage jobs from their counterparts on the Democrat and Republican Parties for endorsements, benefitting friends and family members, and by merely a stroke of a pen by one of those Conservative Party Leaders those Democrat and Republican candidates were also on the Conservative Party Line. Yes, I believe there was a "quid pro qou" transaction, financed by New York State Taxpayers.

I attended a sham Suffolk County Conservative Party convention in the 1990s. During the proceedings, a motion was made to waive the roll call vote and proceed with a voice vote. Even though those opposing the motion were clearly louder than those in support, the chairman declared, "The ayes have it." I witnessed a similar situation at a Republican Party of Virginia convention in 2015, and comparable incidents were broadcast on national television during a Democratic Convention in 2016.

The most frightening experience that I had involved a candidate I supported, despite disagreeing with him on his involvement in an Unidentified Flying Object Network group, which he led. However, he aligned with the principles of the Conservative Party of New York/Suffolk County and stood in opposition to a pro-abortion Democrat who had been endorsed by the Chairman of the Suffolk County Conservative Party.

At that time, I was busy gathering signatures for my nominating petition to secure ballot access and force a Conservative Party Primary against another candidate I did not consider a true conservative. Because I was unable to collect signatures for him myself, I asked my friend and political mentor, Dan Fenessey, to deliver the nominating petitions for John Ford in his mailbox.

The very next day, John Ford was arrested and accused of attempting to inject radioactive isotopes into the toothpaste and other personal items of Suffolk County Republican Party Chairman John Powell. My name appeared on the "Committee to Fill Vacancies," meaning that if he gained ballot access, the "Committee to Fill Vacancies" could select another candidate to run for that public office.

In my view, the allegations presented by the Suffolk County District Attorney against John Ford were, in effect, aimed at me, as I was actively attempting to gain control of the Suffolk County Conservative Party from the corrupt individuals who controlled it. I was interviewed by Long Island's News Station News 12, and, although I did not believe the charges were legitimate, I publicly denounced such actions as not reflective of Conservative values nor the Conservative Party.

At that time, I was employed at Brookhaven National Laboratory. I later learned that the laboratory conducted an inventory of all radioactive material (RAM). Although I had no access to such materials, I was relieved to learn that all radioactive inventory was fully accounted for.

The District Attorney who charged John Ford, Suffolk County District Attorney James Caterson, was described as highly corrupt in the late Henry Hyde's book, "Forfeiting our Property Rights." I believed there was no possibility the prosecution would succeed, and I was ultimately proven correct. Instead of pursuing a conviction, the District Attorney arranged for Mr. Ford to be committed to a mental institution, where he spent over 30 years.

Meanwhile, John Powell was later convicted of operating an illegal chop shop involving stolen automobiles and parts and accepting kickbacks from companies to dump Hazardous material in the Brookhaven Town Landfill. Mr. Powell ultimately died in prison from a heart attack while preparing for a comeback.

This, in my view, reflects the corruption within the Republican Party of New York, one of the two corrupt political parties I have opposed.

Not to be outdone in the corruption arena is the New York Democratic Party. Its Speaker of the General Assembly, Sheldon Silvers, was convicted on federal corruption charges for accepting over $4 million in bribes. More recently, Governor Andrew Cuomo faced allegations of sexual harassment.

This is why I oppose big government, as it often leads to even greater corruption. I am particularly envious of France, where the media provides more equal access to all political parties, helping to limit the dominance of the two majors and often corrupt political powers.

At the Republican Party of Virginia State in 2015, I proposed a resolution to allow registration by political party and to implement closed primaries limited only to registered party members. This effort was intended to prevent individuals like Donald Trump, who had been a lifelong democrat at the time, from influencing the party's nomination process.

I also witnessed what I consider corruption within the Republican Party of Virginia. During my time as a member, there were individuals who contributed to the Democrat Senatorial Campaign Committee and the Democratic Congressional Campaign Committee in 2008. Those actions helped enable the Democratic Party to gain control of the US House of Representatives, the US Senate, and the Presidency, achieving a filibuster-proof majority.

That majority ultimately led to the passage of the misnamed "Affordable Care Act," which, in my view, increased the cost of healthcare without receiving a single Republican vote.

With the exception of Congressman Thomas Massie, many Republicans have embraced Donald Trump and aligned themselves with him, the "Teflon Don." Congressman Massie successfully repelled a primary challenge from a Trump-endorsed Republican candidate. I refer to such candidates as "Trumplicans," individuals who take, or claim they will take, an oath to the Constitution of the United States while effectively pledging their allegiance to Donald Trump instead.

In Virginia, any registered voter may participate in any party's primary. However, the Republican Party of Virginia requires all candidates to support fellow Republicans and avoid criticizing one another, particularly Donald Trump, even when those individuals, in my view, undermine the US Constitution and the constitutional rights of American citizens.

In 2015, I proposed a resolution at the Republican Party of Virginia State Convention aimed at preventing a lifelong Democrat, Donald J. Trump, from influencing the party's nomination process. Trump had previously contributed to the Democrat Senatorial Committee and the Democratic Congressional Campaign Committee in 2008, a cycle that resulted in Democratic control of the US House of Representatives, the US Senate, and the election of Barack Obama, which ultimately led to the passage of the Affordable Care Act, AKA "Obamacare," without a single Republican Vote. My Resolution, to allow registration by political party, passed overwhelmingly, without any "nay" votes.

Unfortunately, legislators in the Virginia House of Delegates and the Virginia State Senate did not introduce any corresponding legislation.

For a more Perfect Union, I believe all political parties should be abolished, and candidates should be elected based on their individual merit and ideas rather than party affiliation. At the city and municipal level, candidates often run on their own merit rather than along party lines, demonstrating that such a system is possible.

In my view, loyalty to any political party, or to any individual, is a form of disloyalty to the Constitution of the United States. When voters in both the Republican and Democratic parties vote blindly along party lines, they grant greater power to political parties at the expense of both their candidates and the Constitution itself.

The USA Is a Constitutional Republic Not a Democracy

The biggest misconception many Americans have, especially the news media, is that the United States government is a "democracy," which was never the case. The United States is a constitutional republic. What separates it from what I describe as "mob rule" is the first ten amendments to the Constitution, commonly known as the Bill of Rights. These amendments are intended to protect individual rights and to limit the power of the federal government, as well as to preserve the balance between federal and state authority.

These rights apply broadly to people within the United States and are foundational to the nation's legal framework. In my view, democracy can become unconstitutional when a majority violates the rights of the minority.

Alexis De Tocqueville, in his classic work, mistitled as it was, "Democracy in America," referred to this as "tyranny of the majority." The Bill of Rights was designed, in part, to guard against such outcomes and to help form a more perfect union.

Separation Of Powers

Many people who voted for Barack Obama in 2008 and 2012 believed they were electing a leader with sweeping authority. In their view, that perception was reinforced when Democrats controlled both houses of Congress and passed the Affordable Care Act, "Obamacare," without a single Republican vote.

Similarly, many who voted for Donald Trump in 2016 and again in 2024 believed they were electing a leader who would exercise strong, centralized power. In my view, this trend intensified when President Trump used executive authority to impose tariffs without direct congressional legislation. Tariffs, as commonly understood in economics, function as taxes.

The US Constitution limits federal power to those authorities specifically granted within it. For example, under the Tenth Amendment to the United States Constitution, powers not delegated to the federal government are reserved to the states or the People. The Constitution does not explicitly grant the federal government authority over broad healthcare legislation. By contrast, states such as Massachusetts enacted their own healthcare systems, for instance, under Governor Mitt Romney, which falls within state authority, that Barack Obama and the Democrats ignored.

Additionally, Article I, Section 8 of the US Constitution grants Congress, not the president, the power to levy taxes. Concentrating such authority in a single individual risks transforming the presidency into something resembling a monarchy. In my view, this reflects a danger of political parties: loyalty often shifts from the constitution to party leadership or individual figures.

Both the Democratic and Republican parties have contributed to the erosion of constitutional principles since the era of the Contract with America, which was enacted by a Republican-controlled Congress and signed by Democratic President William Jefferson Clinton. Since then, the national debt has grown to almost $40 trillion, placing a significant burden on future generations.

I believe it is time to reconsider the two-party system, either by eliminating political parties altogether, as was the case when the

Constitution was first ratified, or by transitioning to a multiparty system that requires broader cooperation for the general good of all citizens and residents.

Finally, I refer to what I call "Judicial Tyranny," sometimes described as "legislating from the bench." When the court. Particularly, the Supreme Court of the United States interprets laws in ways that effectively alter their meaning; it can be seen as rewriting legislation passed by Congress and signed by the President. For example, in cases involving the Affordable Care Act, the Court addressed gaps in the law regarding state healthcare marketplaces and subsidies. In my view, when legislation is flawed or unconstitutional, courts should return it to the legislative body for correction, regardless of which party controls it. A Democrat Congress passed the ACA, a Republican Controlled Congress should have had the opportunity to change it, NOT the Supreme Court.

If political parties did not dominate the legislative process, such conflicts might be less pronounced. In that sense, reforming or rethinking the role of parties could contribute to a more perfect union.

Constitutional Amendments to Be Repealed

Prohibition was enacted by the **18th Amendment** to the Constitution and repealed by the **21st Amendment** to the Constitution because it proved to be a bad law. As Sir Edmund Burke famously stated, *"Bad laws are the worst form of tyranny."*

In a similar vein, two other amendments warrant reconsideration:

1- The 16th Amendment allows the federal government to tax the income of Americans.

2- The 17th Amendment requires Senators to be elected directly by the people rather than by the state.

The 16th Amendment can be seen as the root of the expansion of the federal government, contributing to the rise of national debt. The 17th Amendment, on the other hand, removed a key mechanism that once protected the rights of the states against increasingly centralized federal authority.

The House of Representatives has traditionally been referred to as the *"People's House,"* as its members are directly elected by the public. However, with Senators also elected by the people, the distinction between the two chambers has diminished. In practice, due to the dominance of the Republican and Democratic Parties, elected officials often represent party interests and leadership rather than the people themselves.

The Founding Fathers recognized the importance of balancing power. They envisioned a system in which:

1- The strongest government authority exists closest to the people, at the city, county, and municipal levels.

2- State governments manage local concerns such as infrastructure and law enforcement.

3- The federal government focuses on national defense, interstate commerce, and foreign policy, areas beyond the effective reach of state and local governments.

This principle is reflected in the 10th Amendment, which was ratified to protect state and local authority from federal overreach.

Chief Justice John Marshal once stated, "The power to tax involves the power to destroy." This idea is often applied to the long-term effects of income taxation on American citizens.

A key question arises: If the income tax were abolished, how would the federal government generate revenue?

Before the 16th Amendment, revenue was primarily raised through taxes on goods and services, imposed by Congress. A national sales tax could serve as an alternative.

I often ask people these questions: How much do prostitutes outside of Nevada, or others involved in criminal activity, such as selling illegal drugs or stolen goods, pay in income tax? The answer is zero. How much do those same individuals pay in state sales tax on goods and services? The answer is that they do pay their applicable state sales tax.

There are several states that have no state income tax and generate revenue solely through state sales. Even a national sales tax as high as 25% on everything we buy could be less burdensome than paying 10% on all of one's earnings.

This system would not be strictly regressive or progressive, as wealthier individuals tend to purchase more expensive goods, such as higher-end automobiles, while those with low-income purchase less expensive items. There would be no need for a luxury tax, only a flat tax. The "Underground" economy would come to the surface, and all residents of the US would pay Federal taxes. The 16th and 17th Amendments should be repealed, just as another bad law, prohibition, was repealed in pursuit of a more perfect union.

Legislation For a More Perfect Union

The Republican and Democratic parties have passed laws and even "entangled "alliances that violated individual rights, states' rights, and the Constitution of the United States. To provide for a more perfect union, I recommend the following legislation and changes within the federal government, presented in order of importance.

A. America's National Debt

President Thomas Jefferson said, "Loading up the nation with debt and leaving it for the following generations to pay is morally irresponsible. Excessive debt is a means by which governments oppress the people and waste their substance. No nation has the right to contract debt for periods longer than the majority contracting it can expect to live."

I believe that when one generation increases the national debt beyond what it can repay and passes it on to future generations yet to be born, it amounts to "taxation without representation," which was a central theme for the American Revolution.

The National Debt is now over $39 Trillion. Barack Obama increased the national debt by $8.36 trillion over eight years, while Donald Trump increased it by $8.18 Trillion during his first four-year term, including $2.26 Trillion in the first year of his second term alone, earning him, in this view, the title "King of Debt." Joe Biden increased the national debt by approximately $6 Trillion.

Over the past 17 years, this two-headed Democrat-Republican system has increased the national debt by $24 trillion out of the total $39 trillion. Both parties, in effect, promote big government.

This plan is not draconian but rather a compassionate approach, necessary to preserve America's constitutional republic for another 250 years. As a former federal employee, I understand that approximately 5% - 7% of the federal workforce retires each year. There are also several federal agencies that are no longer necessary or whose functions overlap with those of state governments, for example, the Department of Education, which does not directly educate children, and the Environmental Protection Agency, despite the existence of similar agencies at the state level.

In any organization, employment represents the highest cost. Instead of laying off federal employees in a drastic way, as was done during the Trump administration, the government should identify positions across all federal agencies that are unnecessary or redundant, and when individuals in those positions retire, they should not be replaced. When positions are not necessary, the Office of Personnel Management should move them to positions in other Federal organizations.

This approach would gradually reduce the size of the federal government by approximately 5% each year at least. As the economy grows, this reduction could contribute to paying down the national debt at a similar annual rate. Not getting involved in unnecessary wars, like the war with Iran, the cost of missiles costing millions of dollars compounded with the loss of two aircraft costing nearly $100 million dollars each, is mortgaging future generations of Americans.

B. Abortion And Taking Care of the Most Vulnerable of Americans

A woman does have a right to choose what she does with her body, but there are limitations: for example, suicide is not considered acceptable. However, as a degreed nuclear engineer, I present a science-based argument against abortion. The DNA of an unborn child is different from that of the mother. This is an inconvenient and irrefutable fact that the unborn child is a separate human being.

For those who support abortion as a right, I argue that it is not a constitutionally protected right. Many who have seen the late Pastor Jerry Falwell's *The Silent Scream* believe it demonstrates the termination of a human life in the womb. I view this as barbaric. The Fifth Amendment to the Constitution of the United States protects the right to life of a "person," and there are those in the Right To Life community who support a constitutional amendment granting "personhood" to an unborn child. However, I am not among them.

To me, it is ludicrous, as someone who has studied science and biology, to conclude that a human being is not a "person." I believe the Founding Fathers who wrote the Constitution would not have reached such a conclusion either.

A girlfriend of mine had sex with her then fiancé, an Egyptian national and son of an Egyptian diplomat, at the age of nineteen and became pregnant. Although her mother urged her to have an abortion, she refused.

This was a difficult burden for her to carry. She and her child experienced significant hardship, as the father returned to Egypt and provided no child support. While I believe she made the right decision in giving birth to her son, I also believe she should have considered adoption, an option that is often overlooked in the abortion debate.

When I was in the US Navy, I had sex with a woman before deployment. A few months later, I received a" Dear John" letter informing me that she had an abortion and that I was not the father. This was the 1980s, before the widespread use of DNA testing. It took me over five years to tell my mother, knowing the question she would ask: "My grandchild?"

To which I replied, "Only God knows!"

Since it takes both a man and a woman to conceive a child, I believe both individuals should have a voice in that decision, not just the woman. In that respect, I consider myself "pro-choice."

I also address the claim that abortion is necessary to save the life of the mother. In my view, there is no medical procedure that requires abortion as a prerequisite to saving the mother's life. If, during the procedure to save the mother, the unborn child does not survive, that is not considered an abortion. In some cases, it may be prudent to deliver the child prematurely, with the technological advances in incubators, which allow a child to develop outside the womb.

The late Supreme Court Justice Sandra Day O'Connor argued that Roe v. Wade was on a "collision course with itself" because advances in medical technology continue to push the point of fetal viability, earlier in pregnancy.

Many years ago, I was asked whether I would support paying a woman to have a child. My immediate response was "YES," and "Adoption is an option." I grew up during a time when missing children were featured on milk cartons. Why would a society abort children when others are being kidnapped? I view this as a supply-and-demand issue that could be addressed.

There are so many churches and organizations that oppose abortion and are willing to support adoptions, despite their high cost. I would support tax credits to help cover the cost of pregnancy and childbirth, along with modest compensation, such as $1,000 for the mother. The goal would not be to encourage pregnancy, but to provide support for those who choose to give birth after an unplanned pregnancy.

This approach could reduce the financial burden on society and the federal government while significantly reducing, if not eliminating, abortions. Providing adoption as a viable option would contribute, in my view, to a more perfect union.

C. Illegal Immigration

The Trump Administration has promoted the idea that Immigration and Customs Enforcement (ICE) and the Department of Homeland Security are targeting "the worst of the worst" criminal illegal immigrants. If that were true, why have operations focused on states and cities led by Democratic mayors and governors? If that were true, why has the federal government raided businesses and arrested employees? If that were the case, why were US citizens being arrested, and why were two US citizens killed, one allegedly armed only with a cell phone and possessing a concealed carry permit? The Virginia Citizens Defense League issued a Press Release condemning the killing of a man who was UNARMED and killed for merely possessing a Concealed Carry Permit.

I saw a skit on *Saturday Night Live* that referred to Kristi Noem as a "Secretary of War" against American citizens. While intended as humor, I find the implication deeply concerning and somewhat accurate.

The truth is that most illegal immigrants come to the United States in search of employment, often hired and exploited by unscrupulous employers. A notable example involves the Trump Organization, where Donald Trump, as Chief Operating Officer, hired Polish illegal immigrants to remove the Commodore Hotel to make room for Trump Tower, and then refused to pay them. Ironically, it was a US Labor Union that took the cheapskate/deadbeat to Civil court to pay them. On the witness stand, micromanager Donald J. Trump stated under oath that he did not hire illegal immigrants. The Jury, by a preponderance of the evidence, concluded that Trump was guilty of hiring those Polish undocumented immigrants for over $1 Million.

Instead of targeting illegal immigrants, target employers like Donald J. Trump and place them in jail for hiring illegal immigrants, I would consider granting illegal immigrants permanent RESIDENT status in the United States, NOT CITIZENSHIP, if they testify against their employers and prosecute them for violating Federal Law. This will reduce illegal immigration, if not eliminate it, without a wall and harassing our people, and even killing them. This would be to secure a more perfect union and to secure our borders.

D. Healthcare

The misnamed "Affordable Care Act" AKA "Obamacare" was an unmitigated disaster as the cost of healthcare has soared, not because of the greed of Insurance Companies, but the greed of lawyers and the legal profession. When the United Kingdom developed its National Healthcare System, it realized that they were being sued such that they could not afford its healthcare system, so it had to cap the damage awards on civil litigation. Unfortunately, we have more Lawyers in this country than we have doctors. The cost for OBGYN Malpractice insurance is the highest, and in Virginia, it is over $62,000 per year. There is a shortage of OBGYNs all across the country because of that. Any healthcare plan should be administered by State Governments, as the 10th Amendment to the Constitution only allows the Federal Government to be involved in areas specifically referenced in the Constitution. Any legislation must cap civil awards to maintain the viability of any healthcare program.

Allow patients to tailor-make a plan specifically for them. A 62-year-old woman does not require pregnancy care, and a man does not need mammograms. Big Pharma must recoup the cost of research and development. Tort reform is essential for any healthcare reform plan, and that would make for a more perfect union.

E. North Atlantic Treaty Organization (NATO)

Though I support the alliance, there are two things about the agreement I strongly oppose: placing United States Forces under FOREIGN Command and requiring the United States to act if any nation is attacked. There is absolutely no reason to allow United States Military forces to fly under the flag of any nation but the USA. In World War II, we coordinated efforts working with the militaries of other nations to win the war. The power to declare war rests with the Congress of the United States, and that requirement is unconstitutional, just as a President waging war without Congressional approval is unconstitutional. This would make for a more perfect union.

F.   Foreign Policy and Border Protection

The United States should withdraw all military forces from around the world. With eleven Aircraft Carriers, we can be anywhere on a day's notice or journey. Relocate troops to our southern border to prevent invaders from South America and Mexico, and stop drugs from entering this country. I was in the US Navy when President Ronald Wilson Reagan was President, and I strongly supported him. I objected to being the Policemen of the world. We need to protect America's Interests alone, and that would make for a more perfect union.

No more foreign aid to any country or supplying military hardware unless it is paid for at cost to the Federal Government. Though I support Israel and Ukraine, using the words of former Libertarian candidate for President and Republican Congressman Ron Paul, "we are broke," and worse than that, we have over $39 trillion in debt. It is irresponsible and immoral to continue to pass on more debt to future generations of Americans to pay for this foreign aid. With China loaning us the money to pay our debt, it is also a National Security risk.

If Ukraine wants our Military technology, like the Patriot Missile System, have the European Union pay us to provide weapons to Ukraine to fight the Evil Empire, Russia.

No more free rides for Israel, either; have other countries pay for the weapons we supply them with. The month I was commissioned, November 1985, Jonathan Pollard was arrested for spying for Isreal and as far as I know, Iran was not able to have an American Citizen spy for them. Also, other countries need to give Israel money, as it is suspected that if the USA does not continue to give Israel economic support, its economy will collapse. The USA may be holding up the Israeli economy, but we cannot continue to do that. on the backs of Americans yet to be born.

Bringing the US Military Home from Foreign Bases, to protect America's borders by land, sea, or Air. We do not need a military as large as the United States Military to protect our borders from illegal immigrants, drug traffickers, or human traffickers. Reducing the size of the US Military will be the easiest part of the Federal Government to cut. The US should stop being the Police for the entire world. America cannot afford it.

No More Federal Slavery

Slavery was abolished when the 14th Amendment was passed, but both Democrats and Republicans in Congress continue to use Federal Employees as Pawns and risk National Security and National Safety to get the other side to give in. Before there is another Federal "shutdown" in which Essential Federal Employees are required to work to protect public safety and National Security, Congress shall pass a law paying all Essential Federal Employees. No More Slavery. I was an Essential Federal Employee during Trump's first term in office and worked without pay for over thirty days, and I considered myself a slave to the Federal Government. Fortunately for myself, I was able to pay my bills because my then wife had the resources to pay our expenses; others were not so fortunate. Congress must act now and pass legislation to pay Essential Federal Employees, as those furloughed can apply for Unemployment through their states, or they can work other jobs to pay their bills. Essential Federal Employees receive nothing unless they work outside their federal hours, and that could adversely affect their ability to perform their Essential Federal job.

John B. Bloom

Defeating Gerrymandering

The most dangerous threat to America's Constitutional Republic is Gerrymandering and the "Two-Party System." When the Constitution of the United States was written and ratified, there was no mention of political parties, as our founders knew that political parties would tear our nation apart. One may wonder why I grouped what has been accepted since the mid 1970's, after other minor political parties threatened the two predominant political parties in the USA, the Democratic and Republican Parties; these two political parties across all 50 states passed legislation, placing barriers for other political parties to operate in their respective states. Gerrymandering can only be effective and thrive in this two-party system that those two parties put in place. Gerrymandering is not effective at all with more than two political parties. Gerrymandering is essential for those two political parties to share power. Any State Commission created for the purpose of redistricting, comprised of members of those two political parties, will not create most of the districts with a near 50% Republican and Democrat split. Rather, the Commission would redistrict state or federal public office districts so that the district is Gerrymandered Republican or Democrat. That would all change when a candidate from another political party is on the ballot, and the News Media provided them equal and fair exposure as Democrat and Republican candidates are.

Then, as many people have so many different beliefs on a variety of issues, how can two political parties provide for such a diversity of positions? They cannot. I am 100% Pro-life, though a former US Navy Officer, serving during the President Ronald Reagan years. I did not like being the Police of the World. As a pro-life, I should be a Republican, but they support being the police of the world. With two political parties, they are diametrically opposite in a myriad of positions. We emphasize diversity in people; why not in political parties? As the Chairman of the Constitution Party of Virginia, I have a party that best represents what I believe. As a recovering republican, I also realize what Republicans and Democrats have been promoting for years, using the "Fear Factor" to manipulate voters into believing one must make a BINARY choice or risk helping someone from the party they "FEAR" may get elected, making it hard for minor political parties to exist.

The 4th Congressional District was gerrymandered by republicans when Republican Congressman Randy Forbes represented the district. Then, when the Democrats controlled both houses of the Virginia Legislature and Terry McAuliffe was Governor, the district was gerrymandered, for a Democrat to win the seat, Congressman Fornes did not run for re-election in that district, and a Democrat has represented that district ever since.

There was a time after the Civil War, when the Republican Party was called the "Black Party," when black men and then black women were allowed to vote. The Civil Rights Act of 1960 was passed with bipartisan support as Republicans and Democrats in the Northern states supported it, while Segregationist Democrats in the Southern States opposed it with Jim Crow era laws restricting the rights of black men and women from voting. With most blacks being in the Democrat Party now, Gerrymandering has been used as a racist tool by Republicans to pack black voters into Congressional Districts, allowing Republicans to gain seats by race. When I moved to Virginia in 2010, I lived in Newport News, where the person I call "Congressman For Life," Bobby Scott, represented. That seat was Gerrymandered at the time and stretched from every black community from Richmond to Norfolk. Now, though the district is still Gerrymandered for Democrats to win, and Congressman Bobby Scott still represents the district, the district is not as badly Gerrymandered as it once was. As a white male, Congressman Bobby Scott has never represented me. Now I live in Spotsylvania County, Virginia, with my girlfriend and though a Democrat represents the district with Congressman Eugene Vindman, a white man, I feel optimistic that I will finally have representation.

I can never comprehend the foolishness of voters. Why would anyone in a Democratic Gerrymandered district vote for a Republican? I ran against a pro-gun control Republican for state Senate in a Democrat Gerrymandered district, in which many in that Senate district voted for me when I ran as a Republican and received the most votes by a republican running in that district, however I received less than 5% of the vote, when I ran for State Senate and the Virginia Citizens Defense League, not only endorsed me, but their Political Action Committee donated towards my campaign and I was probably more grateful for their donation than anyone else.

To combat this manipulation by the Republican and Democratic Parties into voting for their "Lesser of Two Evils" candidates, and to allow diversity in political parties and to make a more perfect union, "rank choice voting" is essential. This would allow a voter to vote for the candidate that best represents them and allow the voter to vote for his 2nd choice to ensure the candidate they want the least gets no votes, where the 1st choice would get 3 "votes" while their 2nd choice would get one vote. The candidate with the most "votes" wins.

"It Is Not Yours to Give"

When Davy Crockett was a congressman, he debated a bill to give taxpayer money to the widow of a man who died in battle, and said to fellow congressmen, "It is not yours to give." As a Christian, I donate to my Church, and for decades I have argued that Churches have abdicated their responsibility to take care of the "poor" to the Federal Government, and taxed its citizens for this purpose, and it was not theirs to give.

There are some religious organizations that lobby the Federal Government for federal funds that must stop. I would allow taxpayers to take tax **credits** for charitable contributions. Unlike the Federal Government and its bloated bureaucracy, charitable organizations have low overhead costs and are augmented by caring volunteers, rather than paid, uncaring employees. Appeal to Churches across the country to provide housing, food, and clothing, and even vocational training, taking back what is rightly the function of churches and getting the uncaring federal Government out of Social programs, as it is not theirs to give.

Social Security Retirement

The Life Expectancy as of 2024 is 79 years in the United States. I would increase the retirement age from 62 years to 72, with maximum benefits at the age of 75, effective in 10 years, so people can plan with their Individual Retirement Accounts and/or their 401 (k). Social Security Retirement was designed to support an individual's retirement income, not as their sole source of retirement income. Once the size of the Federal Government is reduced, the National Debt, which is deferred taxation passed onto future generations, and taxation on the American people will be reduced, allowing them to save for their future when they retire. The current generation and future generations of Americans have been taxed to the debt, and that must stop. No more taxing Social Security Retirement Income and no longer reducing Social Security Income by exceeding an arbitrary limit. Those on Social Security work to cover the gap between their income and expenses and should not be penalized for working.

Civil Discord

The United States of America needs to start having elections that are "civil" with running "clean" campaigns based on expertise and knowledge. ideas and solutions, in lieu of monetary advantages or disadvantages. The media has the responsibility, as set forth in the 1st Amendment, to have open debates, giving all candidates, regardless of political party affiliation. It has always been a minority of individuals that developed the light bulb, the telephone, and the radio; ignoring the views of individuals that are not Republican or Democrat is a disservice to the American people and detrimental to being a more perfect union. In France not too long ago, the French media gave equal time to all political parties, including one that was less than a year old and resulted in the jettison of both political parties that were in power at the time and elected Emanuel Macron, from that newly formed party, oh how I envy the French people and long for the American media to do as the French media did. My girlfriend shared these ideas with me, we require amenable agreements based on contractual agreements and open discussion and debate put into place that will benefit both the Republican and Democrat Parties, and for the benefit of we the people. Providing useful information and sharing of ideas equally and resolutions, preventions, and provisions, that will help to resolve past issues, prevent future issues, and provide for a more perfect union for our country.

John B. Bloom

The Electoral College and A Convention Article V Constitutional Convention

Our Founding Fathers created a unique system to elect the President and Vice-President the United States, and protect the American people from electing a King or Dictator in the Electoral College. The number of Electors assigned to the states is based on the number of Congressional representatives a state is assigned, based on a state's population, plus one elector for each of the two US Senators. As an example, Virginia, the state I live in, is assigned 11 Congressional Representatives and, of course, 2 US Senators; therefore, Virginia has 13 Electors.

Most states, like Virginia, are winner-take-all states. Though an elector can vote for any candidate, most states require Electors to vote for the candidate that wins the state, and also the Designating Petitions for a candidate for President/Vice-President include the names of all electors. All Electors for the Republican and Democratic candidates for the ticket would be loyal to that political party, if not party officers, in that state.

In 2016, when I was a Republican, I tried to get those who disliked Hillary Clinton to vote for Constitution Party nominee Darrel Castle, as I knew Donald J. Trump would not win Virginia, as the real wasted vote in Virginia was a vote for Trump, as one would not have to compromise on what they believed in, to vote for Mr. Castle. Mr. Castle wound up with the same number of electoral votes as Trump did, zero.

In other states, Hillary Clinton stood no chance of winning RED States like Oklahoma, but instead of working with alternative political parties, like the Libertarian or Constitution Parties, they did not have Clinton on the ballot in those states, while promoting one of them. On the flip side, Republicans had no chance of winning big Blue States, like California, and not run Trump in those states and promote the Green Party nominee. With that competition, that Presidential election would have been totally up for grabs. In 2024, the Democrats ran their candidates for President/Vice-President (Harris/Walz) in RED States where they had no chance of winning. I blame the Democrats for the election of Donald J. Trump in both 2016 and 2024. The Electoral System and viable alternatives to the Republican and Democratic parties would have prevented the election of a Dictator wannabe.

Under no circumstances is an Article V Constitutional Convention. The US Constitution is fine; however, both the Republican and Democratic Parties have not been following the Constitution for decades, resulting in an Unconstitutional Federal Government. In addition, Congress sets the rules for the Constitutional Convention, including the number of delegates for each state, and most, if not all, delegates would be Democratic or Republican party officers and could be publicly elected officials from those two political parties. That is like having the wolf "guard" the hen house. In the words of my favorite talk show host, WNIS Radio, Norfolk, Virginia, Tony Macrini, "We do not have any Thomas Jeffersons or John Adams now; we could lose everything." The last time we had a Constitutional Convention was when the Articles of Confederation were to be modified, which resulted in scrapping the Articles of Confederation and resulting in a new form of government in the Constitution of the United States.

A Constitutional Convention risks scrapping the Constitution of the United States and replacing it with a Communist form of Government and losing our individual rights protected by the "Bill of Rights" of the Constitution of the United States.

For A More Perfect Union - The Case for Impeaching Donald J. Trump

Impeachment is a civil action and not a criminal one. The level of proof is merely preponderance of the evidence and not beyond a reasonable doubt, nor is there any statute of limitations on any prior act. Can anyone be above the law? Should anyone above the law be allowed to continue as President? Below are the facts of the actions of Donald J. Trump:

1. In the 1980's, he was found liable and guilty of hiring illegal Polish Immigrants to remove the Commodore Hotel to make room for him to build Trump Tower on that spot and paid a judgment of $1 Million by preponderance of the evidence.

2. He stated under oath that he did not know he hired undocumented immigrants, which I contend was a flagrant LIE in which the jury agreed with me and awarded those workers $1 Million, and he was not charged criminally for violating Federal Law.

3. In the 1990s, he allegedly sexually assaulted E. Jean Carroll, who was awarded over $88 Million for two Sexual Assaults.

4. Though Donald J. Trump has over 5,300 files and references in the Epstein files, in which major expansion of Federal Power and the passage of the misnamed "Affordable Care Act" AKA "OBAMACARE" without a single Republican vote, which led to skyrocketing healthcare costs.

5. If there is evidence of sexual misconduct, the Statute of Limitations for any sexual assault accusations has long passed.

6. Though this is not a crime and the media suppressed this information from being disseminated in 2008, Donald J Trump contributed to Crooked Hillary Clinton's Presidential Campaign, the Democratic Senatorial Campaign Committee, and the Democratic Congressional Campaign Committee, which led to Democrats gaining control of both Houses of Congress and the Presidency with a PHILIBUSTER PROOF Senate.

7. Ordering Federal Agencies, ICE, and the office of Homeland Security into cities that resulted in the deaths of U.S. citizens and the arrest of law-abiding accused of being illegal immigrants.

8. Article I, Section 8 of the Constitution authorized Congress to lay and collect taxes, and anyone who has taken an economics class knows that tariffs are taxes; therefore, Donald Trump violated the Constitution and acts more like a king, not a President.

9. Congress has the Power to Declare War and a President does not have the Constitutional Authority to attack another country without Congressional approval, again, actions that are more consistent with a KING than a President of the United States.

10. The Trump administration may have committed a war crime by firing upon foreign military members after the ship they were on was no longer a threat and were defenseless.

Though I ran on the Libertarian Party line last year and had the courage to criticize Donald Trump, the Republican Party of Virginia can stop me from running on the Republican Party line. Donald J. Trump faced no consequences when he helped finance the Democrat Takeover of Congress and the Presidency.

11. He was convicted of 32 Felony Counts in a New York State Court that included overvaluing his properties to obtain favorable Loan terms, yet undervaluing the same properties to pay less taxes. Is that Mortgage Fraud, Tax evasion, or both? The New York State Supreme Court, instead of deferring sentencing until Donald J. Trump is no longer President of the United States, set aside sentencing, talking about being above the law.

12. All the checks shown in that New York State court case were payable to Trump's then "Fixer," Michael Cohen, for alleged payments to Porn Star Stormy Daniels that had Mr. Cohen being incarcerated, yet the person who benefited from all of this action was Donald J. Trump.

13. Renovating the White House, which is a Historic Landmark, without Congressional Approval.

14. Removing classified documents from the White House and storing them in a nonsecure location at his Mar-Largo residence. If anyone else did that, they would have spent time in Federal Prison for at the very least mishandling classified material.

15. Being instrumental in the attempted Insurrection of the Capitol building that led to the death of Capitol Police and Civilians loyal to Donald Trump and NOT the Constitution of the United States. That led to

the deaths of several individuals, including several Washington, D.C., police officers who were protecting members of Congress

16. Attacking another country and kidnapping the leader of another country, both without provocation, justification, and without Congressional approval, in violation of Article 1 of the US Constitution, which grants Congress the power to declare war, on another country.

It is essential for America's Constitutional Republic to survive that the Constitution of the United States be more powerful than any President and to ensure a President is NOT a KING.

No man is above the law, and having a lawbreaker as President who has violated several Federal and State laws as well as the Constitution of the United States is an embarrassment, a man I refer to as "The First Felon." To make a More Perfect Union, Donald J. Trump must be.

Resources:

Letters to Editor I wrote that were published in Newspapers across the country:

https://drive.google.com/drive/folders/0B59EKzgU-7F3fldmOGVtdDFZcE1yRmdGYXJVY0VzbjAxS2pJOGxtbktDSWpiUGxVeEFocTQ?resourcekey=0-WIkCbt3KRIYR6GyrbZeVXg&usp=sharing

The Silent Scream:

https://upload.wikimedia.org/wikipedia/commons/transcoded/2/27/The_Silent_Scream_%281984%29.ogg/The_Silent_Scream_%281984%29.ogg.360p.webm

E. Jean Caroll V Donald Trump:

https://en.wikipedia.org/wiki/E._Jean_Carroll_v._Donald_J._Trump

Donald Trump used Illegal Immigrants to build Trump Tower and REFUSED to Pay Them:

https://www.presidency.ucsb.edu/documents/rubio-campaign-press-release-fact-check-donald-trump-used-illegal-immigrants-build-trump

President does not have Constitutional Authority to lay and collect taxes:

https://www.pierceatwood.com/alerts/federal-trade-court-rules-trump-lacks-authority-tariffs-under-ieepa

Attack on Venezuela is Unconstitutional:

https://www.brennancenter.org/our-work/analysis-opinion/attack-venezuela-was-unconstitutional

CARENET

https://care-net.org/ - A PRO-ABUNDANT LIFE MINISTRY

GRACEFUL ADOPTIONS

https://gracefuladoptions.com/

HOW TO ADOPT

https://howtoadopt.org/

CENTER for ADOPTION SUPPORT AND EDUCATION

https://adoptionsupport.org/

FAMILY RAISING

https://wearefamiliesrising.org/adoption-assistance/virginia-adoption-assistance-program/

ADOPT VIRGINIA

https://www.dss.virginia.gov/nam/post_adoption_service_search.html

Text of the Constitution of the United States:

https://constitutioncenter.org/the-constitution/full-text?gad_source=1&gad_campaignid=21248037516&gbraid=0AAAAADJbFsCZ3JS8pzRQRnLJAuCb6I4PI&gclid=CjwKCAiAqKbMBhBmEiwAZ3UboDrVPhiWocRvQb0JHxh9oBczhwcGZj24PW7ADkNvbHvxCoU40In_2BoCXh4QAvD_BwE